FAVOURITE POEMS OF
BANJO PATERSON

PAINTINGS BY REX NEWELL

FAVOURITE POEMS OF
BANJO PATERSON

PAINTINGS BY REX NEWELL

INTRODUCTION BY
BRUCE ELDER

NATIONAL
BOOK DISTRIBUTORS AND PUBLISHERS

*I greatly appreciate the time and effort that
has gone into researching material for this
book by the ex-jackeroo, ex-shearer, ex-drover
and good mate of mine,* Cec Baker.

—Rex Newell—

Front cover: "The Man from Snowy River", page 8.
Half-title page: "The Song of the Wheat", page 10.
Page two: "Mulga Bill's Bicycle", page 24.
Back cover: "The Swagman's Rest", page 46.

Published by National Book Distributors and Publishers Pty Ltd
3/2 Aquatic Drive, Frenchs Forest, NSW 2086
First edition 1994
Illustrations © Rex Newell 1994
© National Book Distributors and Publishers Pty Ltd 1994
Introduction by Bruce Elder
Electronic composition by Murray Child and Company
Designed by Emma Seymour
Stunt man for "Mulga Bill's Bicycle" was Alan Bailey
Electronic colour separation and film by Typescan, Adelaide
Printed in Singapore by Cho Jock Min

National Library of Australia Cataloguing-in-Publication data

Paterson, A.B. (Andrew Barton), 1864–1941.
Favourite poems of Banjo Paterson.

ISBN 1 86436 019 4.

I. Newell, Rex, 1938– . II. Title.

A821.2

CONTENTS

INTRODUCTION

Andrew Barton Paterson

The greatness of Andrew Barton "Banjo" Paterson lies in his ability to evoke a world which is uniquely Australian. He is part of every Australian's personal landscape. A poet who captured characters, moments and events which are now part of our national consciousness. Many people have written bush ballads which tell of the adventures and exploits of those brave early settlers who carved farms and towns out of the grey-green bushlands of Australia, but no one managed to tell the stories with as much wit and humour as "The Banjo".

All Australians can relate to the triumph of the wiry little bushman and his horse in *The Man from Snowy River*. It is one of the greatest statements about our love of the underdog. We all admire *The Man from Ironbark* because we too would like to scare the living daylights out of the smart alecs and practical jokers who take advantage of us.

Every Australian believes that when honour and sport are wound together, particularly when it is a case of the snobs versus the ordinary people, that we would stay on the sports field until death rather than let the smooth-talking "yuppies" win. That is why we love *The Geebung Polo Club* so much.

And, of course, there is no greater statement of the way Australians want to see themselves than our unofficial national anthem, *Waltzing Matilda*. It is much more than just the tale of a swaggie who steals a sheep. It is an expression of our dislike of bullying and authority figures. The swaggie is every Australian who ever wanted to laugh in the face of a petty official or stick up a finger at a bullying politician. Somehow, deep in our national consciousness, we are always on the side of the man who steals the sheep. We can never be on the side of the squatter or the troopers. They are the forces we must fight. Better to jump into the billabong than to let these people rule our lives.

These are timeless poems. They tell us, through humour and light-heartedness, about ourselves and about the kind of people Australians really are. They may have been written a century ago but, like all enduring literature, they do not belong to the time of their creation. They say things which are eternally true. They are expressions of the rich and fascinating life that "Banjo" Paterson had.

He was a well-educated man, a lawyer by profession, who was born at the "Narrambla" property near Orange on 17 February 1864. His parents were property owners, but not wealthy squatters or social climbers. In fact his mother moved from the family property "Buckinbah" to "Narrambla" for the birth of young Andrew because "Buckinbah" was too rough and isolated.

When he was about ten years old, Paterson moved to Sydney where he was educated at Sydney Grammar School. All his life he was fascinated with horses. While he studied to become a lawyer he regularly played polo and rode, as an amateur, at both Randwick and Rosehill racecourses.

His first poem appeared in *The Bulletin* on 28 February 1885. A decade later his reputation was such that his first book of poems, *The Man from Snowy River and Other Verses*, when it was published by Angus & Robertson, was sold out before it was even available in the bookshops.

From that point onwards he became a full-time writer working as a war correspondent during the Boer War and the Boxer Rebellion in China, editing the *Evening News* and the *Sydney Sportsman*, and writing for *The Bulletin* and *Smith's Weekly* as well as dozens of other newspapers and magazines.

Although much of his life was spent in Sydney, Paterson never lost his love of horses or his passion for the Australian bush. His childhood experiences had defined him and he was a willing prisoner of those early memories. In this sense he became a symbol of an idea of Australia which has never really disappeared.

We may be one of the most urbanised countries in the world, and over 80 per cent of Australians may live in cities, but our heart, like Paterson's, is still forever there in rural Australia with dusty roads, old shacks of wood and corrugated iron, simple honest people, impossibly blue skies and the endless grey-green of the gumtrees. "Banjo" Paterson captured this mixture of rural and urban for us all and for that he will remain forever at the centre of the real Australian experience.

The combination of Rex Newell's evocative paintings and watercolours and Banjo Paterson's timeless poems will delight everyone who wishes to renew their experience with these unique depictions of Australian life.

THE MAN FROM SNOWY RIVER

There was movement at the station, for the word had passed around
That the colt from old Regret had got away,
And had joined the wild bush horses—he was worth a thousand pound,
So all the cracks had gathered to the fray.
All the tried and noted riders from the stations near and far
Had mustered at the homestead overnight,
For the bushmen love hard riding where the wild bush horses are,
And the stock-horse snuffs the battle with delight.

There was Harrison, who made his pile when Pardon won the cup,
The old man with his hair as white as snow;
But few could ride beside him when his blood was fairly up—
He would go wherever horse and man could go.
And Clancy of the Overflow came down to lend a hand,
No better horseman ever held the reins;
For never horse could throw him while the saddle girths would stand,
He learnt to ride while droving on the plains.

And one was there, a stripling on a small and weedy beast,
He was something like a racehorse undersized,
With a touch of Timor pony—three parts thoroughbred at least—
And such as are by mountain horsemen prized.
He was hard and tough and wiry—just the sort that won't say die—
There was courage in his quick impatient tread;
And he bore the badge of gameness in his bright and fiery eye,
And the proud and lofty carriage of his head.

But so slight and weedy, one would doubt his power to stay,
And the old man said, "That horse will never do
For a long and tiring gallop—lad, you'd better stop away,
Those hills are far too rough for such as you."
So he waited sad and wistful—only Clancy stood his friend—
"I think we ought to let him come," he said;
"I warrant he'll be with us when he's wanted at the end,
For both his horse and he are mountain bred.

"He hails from Snowy River, up by Kosciusko's side,
Where the hills are twice as steep and twice as rough,
Where a horse's hoofs strike firelight from the flint stones every stride,
The man that holds his own is good enough.
And the Snowy River riders on the mountains make their home,
Where the river runs those giant hills between;
I have seen full many horsemen since I first commenced to roam,
But nowhere yet such horsemen have I seen."

So he went—they found the horses by the big mimosa clump—
They raced away towards the mountain's brow,
And the old man gave his orders, "Boys, go at them from the jump,
No use to try for fancy riding now.
And, Clancy, you must wheel them, try and wheel them to the right.
Ride boldly, lad, and never fear the spills,
For never yet was rider that could keep the mob in sight,
If once they gain the shelter of those hills."

So Clancy rode to wheel them—he was racing on the wing
Where the best and boldest riders take their place,
And he raced his stockhorse past them, and he made the ranges ring
With stockwhip, as he met them face to face.
Then they halted for a moment, while he swung the dreaded lash,
But they saw their well-loved mountain full in view,
And they charged beneath the stockwhip with a sharp and sudden dash,
And off into the mountain scrub they flew.

Then fast the horsemen followed, where the gorges deep and black
Resounded to the thunder of their tread,
And the stockwhips woke the echoes, and they fiercely answered back
From cliffs and crags that beetled overhead.
An upward, ever upward, the wild horses held their sway,
Where mountain ash and kurrajong grew wide;
And the old man muttered fiercely, "We may bid the mob good day,
No man can hold them down the other side."

When they reached the mountain's summit, even Clancy took a pull,
It well might make the boldest hold their breath,
The wild hop scrub grew thickly, and the hidden ground was full
Of wombat holes, and any slip was death.
But the man from Snowy River let the pony have his head,
And he swung his stockwhip round and gave a cheer,
And he raced him down the mountain like a torrent down its bed,
While the others stood and watched in very fear.

He sent the flint stones flying, but the pony kept his feet,
He cleared the fallen timbers in his stride,
And the man from Snowy River never shifted in his seat—
It was grand to see that mountain horseman ride.
Through the stringybarks and saplings, on the rough and broken ground,
Down the hillside at a racing pace he went;
And he never drew the bridle till he landed safe and sound,
At the bottom of that terrible descent.

He was right among the horses as they
climbed the further hill
And the watchers on the moun-
tain standing mute,
Saw him ply the stockwhip
fiercely, he was right
among them still,
As he raced across
the clearing
in pursuit.

Then they lost him for a moment, where two mountain gullies met
In the ranges, but a final glimpse reveals
On a dim and distant hillside the wild horses racing yet,
With the man from Snowy River at their heels.

And he ran them single-handed till their sides were white with foam.
He followed like a bloodhound in their track,
Till they halted cowed and beaten, then he turned their heads for
    home,
And alone and unassisted brought them back.
But his hardy mountain pony he could scarcely raise a trot,
He was blood from hip to shoulder from the spur;

But his pluck was still undaunted, and his courage fiery hot,
For never yet was mountain horse a cur.

And down by Kosciusko, where the pine clad ridges raise
Their torn and rugged battlements on high,
Where the air is clear as crystal, and the white stars fairly blaze
At midnight in the cold and frosty sky,
And where around The Overflow the reed beds sweep and sway
To the breezes, and the rolling plains are wide,
The man from Snowy River is a household word today,
And the stockmen tell the story of his ride.

SONG OF THE WHEAT

We have sung the song of the droving days,
    Of the march of the travelling sheep;
By silent stages and lonely ways
    Thin, white battlions creep.
But the man who now by the land would thrive
    Must his spurs to a ploughshare beat.
Is there ever a man in the world alive
    To sing the song of the Wheat!

It's west by south of the Great Divide
    The grim grey plains run out,
Where the old flock masters lived and died
    In a ceaseless fight with drought.
Weary with waiting and hope deferred
    They were ready to own defeat,
Till at last they heard the master-word
    And the master-word was Wheat.

Yarran and Myall and Box and Pine—
    'Twas axe and fire for all;
They scarce could tarry to blaze the line
    Or wait for the trees to fall,
Ere the team was yoked and the gates flung wide,
    And the dust of the horses' feet
Rose up like a pillar of smoke to guide
    The wonderful march of Wheat.

Furrow by furrow, and fold by fold,
    The soil is turned on the plain;
Better than silver and better than gold
    Is the surface-mine of the grain.
Better than cattle and better than sheep
    In the fight with the drought and heat.
For a streak of stubbornness wide and deep
    Lies hid in a grain of Wheat.

When the stock is swept by the hand of fate,
   Deep down in his bed of clay
The brave brown Wheat will lie and wait
   For the resurrection day:
Lie hid while the whole world thinks him dead;
   But the spring rain, soft and sweet,
Will over the steaming paddocks spread
   The first green flush of the Wheat.

Green and amber and gold it grows
   When the sun sinks late in the West
And the breeze sweeps over the rippling rows
   Where the quail and the skylark nest.
Mountain or river or shining star,
   There's never a sight can beat—
Away to the skyline stretching far—
   A sea of the ripening Wheat.

When the burning harvest sun sinks low,
   And the shadows stretch on the plain,
The roaring strippers come and go
   Like ships on a sea of grain;
Till the lurching, groaning waggons bear
   Their tale of the load complete.
Of the world's great work he has done his share
   Who has gathered a crop of wheat.

Princes and Potentates and Czars,
   They travel in regal state,
But old King Wheat has a thousand cars
   For his trip to the water-gate;
And his thousand steamships breast the tide
   And plough thro' the wind and sleet
To the lands where the teeming millions bide
   That say, "Thank God for Wheat!"

SHEARING AT CASTLEREAGH

The bell is set aringing, and the engine gives a toot,
There's five and thirty shearers here are shearing for the loot,
So stir yourselves, you penners-up and shove the sheep along,
The musterers are fetching them a hundred thousand strong,
And make your collie dogs speak up—what would the buyers say
In London if the wool was late this year from Castlereagh?

The man that "rung" the Tubbo shed is not the ringer here,
That stripling from the Cooma side can teach him how to shear.
They trim away the ragged locks, and rip the cutter goes,
And leaves a track of snowy fleece from brisket to the nose;
It's lovely how they peel it off with never stop nor stay,
They're racing for the ringer's place this year at Castlereagh.

The man that keeps the cutters sharp is growling in his cage,
He's always in a hurry and he's always in a rage—
"You clumsy-fisted muttonheads, you'd turn a fellow sick,
You pass yourselves as shearers? You were born to swing a pick!
Another broken cutter here, that's two you've broke today,
It's awful how such crawlers come to shear at Castlereagh."

The youngsters picking up the fleece enjoy the merry din,
They throw the classer up the fleece, he throws it to the bin;
The pressers standing by the rack are waiting for the wool,
There's room for just a couple more, the press is nearly full;
Now jump upon the lever, lads, and heave and heave away,
Another bale of golden fleece is branded "Castlereagh".

THE MAN FROM IRONBARK

It was the man from Ironbark who struck the Sydney town,
He wandered over street and park, he wandered up and down.
He loitered here, he loitered there, till he was like to drop,
Until at last in sheer despair he sought a barber's shop.
" 'Ere! shave my beard and whiskers off, I'll be a man of mark,
I'll go and do the Sydney toff up home in Ironbark."

The barber man was small and flash, as barbers mostly are,
He wore a strike-your-fancy sash, he smoked a huge cigar:
He was a humorist of note and keen at repartee,
He laid the odds and kept a "tote", whatever that may be,
And when he saw our friend arrive, he whispered "Here's a lark!
Just watch me catch him all alive, this man from Ironbark."

There were some gilded youths that sat along the barber's wall.
Their eyes were dull, their heads were flat, they had no brains at all;
To them the barber passed the wink, his dexter eyelid shut,
"I'll make this bloomin' yokel think his bloomin' throat is cut."
And as he soaped and rubbed it in he made a rude remark:
"I s'pose the flats is pretty green up there in Ironbark."

A grunt was all reply he got; he shaved the bushman's chin,
Then made the water boiling hot and dipped the razor in.
He raised his hand, his brow grew black, he paused awhile to gloat,
Then slashed the red-hot razor-back across his victim's throat;
Upon the newly-shaven skin it made a livid mark—
No doubt it fairly took him in—the man from Ironbark.

He fetched a wild up-country yell might wake the dead to hear,
And though his throat, he knew full well, was cut from ear to ear,
He struggled gamely to his feet, and faced the murd'rous foe:
"You've done for me! you dog, I'm beat! one hit before I go!
I only wish I had a knife, you blessed murdering shark!
But you'll remember all your life, the man from Ironbark."

He lifted up his hairy paw, with one tremendous clout
He landed on the barber's jaw, and knocked the barber out.
He set to work with tooth and nail, he made the place a wreck;
He grabbed the nearest gilded youth, and tried to break his neck.
And all the while his throat he held to save his vital spark,
And "Murder! Bloody Murder!" yelled the man from Ironbark.

A peeler man who heard the din came in to see the show;
He tried to run the bushman in, but he refused to go.
And when at last the barber spoke, and said " 'Twas all in fun—
'Twas just a little harmless joke, a trifle overdone."
"A joke!" he cried, "By George, that's fine; a lively sort of lark;
I'd like to catch that murdering swine some night in Ironbark."

And now while round the shearing floor the list'ning shearers gape,
He tells the story o'er and o'er, and brags of his escape.
"Them barber chaps what keeps a tote, By George, I've had enough.
One tried to cut my bloomin' throat, but thank the Lord it's tough."
And whether he's believed or no, there's one thing to remark,
That flowing beards are all the go way up in Ironbark.

IN THE DROVING DAYS

"Only a pound," said the auctioneer,
"Only a pound; and I'm standing here
Selling this animal, gain or loss.
Only a pound for the drover's horse;
One of the sort that was never afraid,
One of the boys of the Old Brigade;
Thoroughly honest and game, I'll swear,
Only a little the worst for wear;
Plenty as bad to be seen in town,
Give me a bid and I'll knock him down;
Sold as he stands, and without recourse,
Give me a bid for the drover's horse."

Loitering there in an aimless way
Somehow I noticed the poor old grey,
Weary and battered and screwed, of course,
Yet when I noticed the old grey horse,
The rough bush saddle, and single rein
Of the bridle laid on his tangled mane,
Straightway the crowd and the auctioneer
Seemed on a sudden to disappear,
Melted away in a kind of haze,
For my heart went back to the droving days.

Back to the road, and I crossed again
Over the miles of the saltbush plain—
The shining plain that is said to be
The dried-up bed of an inland sea,
Where the air so dry and so clear and bright
Refracts the sun with a wondrous light,
And out in the dim horizon makes
The deep blue gleam of the phantom lakes.

At dawn of day we would feel the breeze
That stirred the boughs of the sleeping trees,
And brought a breath of the fragrance rare
That comes and goes in that scented air;
For the trees and grass and the shrubs contain
A dry sweet scent on the saltbush plain.
For those that love it and understand,
The saltbush plain is a wonderland.
A wondrous country, where Nature's ways
Were revealed to me in the droving days.

We saw the fleet wild horses pass,
And the kangaroos through the Mitchell grass,
The emu ran with her frightened brood
All unmolested and unpursued.
But there rose a shout and a wild hubbub
When the dingo raced for his native scrub,
And he paid right dear for his stolen meals
With the drover's dogs at his wretched heels.
For we ran him down at a rattling pace,
While the packhorse joined in the stirring chase.
And a wild halloo at the kill we'd raise—
We were light of heart in the droving days.

'Twas a drover's horse, and my hand again
Made a move to close on a fancied rein.
For I felt the swing and the easy stride
Of the grand old horse that I used to ride
In drought or plenty, in good or ill,
That same old steed was my comrade still;
The old grey horse with his honest ways
Was a mate to me in the droving days.

A BUSHMAN'S SONG

I'm travellin' down the Castlereagh, and I'm a station hand,
I'm handy with the ropin' pole, I'm handy with the brand,
And I can ride a rowdy colt, or swing the axe all day,
But there's no demand for a station-hand along the Castlereagh.

So it's shift, boys, shift, for there isn't the slightest doubt
That we've got to make a shift to the stations further out,
With the packhorse runnin' after, for he follows like a dog,
We must strike across the country at the old jig-jog.

This old black horse I'm riding—if you'll notice what's his brand,
He wears the crooked R, you see—none better in the land.
He takes a lot of beatin', and the other day we tried,
For a bit of a joke, with a racing bloke, for twenty pounds aside.

It was shift, boys, shift, for there wasn't the slightest doubt,
That I had to make him shift, for the money was nearly out;
But he cantered home a winner, with the other one at the flog—
He's a red-hot sort to pick up with his old jig-jog.

I asked a cove for shearin' once along the Marthaguy:
"We shear non-union here," says he. "I call it scab," says I.
I looked along the shearin' floor before I turned to go—
There were eight or ten dashed Chinamen a-shearin' in a row.

It was shift, boys, shift, for there wasn't the slightest doubt
It was time to make a shift with the leprosy about.
So I saddled up my horses, and I whistled to my dog,
And I left his scabby station at the old jig-jog.

I went to Illawarra, where my brother's got a farm,
He has to ask his landlord's leave before he lifts his arm;
The landlord owns the countryside—man, woman, dog, and cat,
They haven't the cheek to dare to speak without they touch their hat.

It was shift, boys, shift, for there wasn't the slightest doubt
Their little landlord god and I would soon have fallen out;
Was I to touch my hat to him?—was I his bloomin' dog?
So I makes for up the country at the old jig-jog.

But it's time that I was movin', I've a mighty way to go
Till I drink artesian water from a thousand feet below;
Till I meet the overlanders with the cattle comin' down,
And I'll work a while till I make a pile, then have a spree in town.

So, it's shift, boys, shift, for there isn't the slightest doubt
We've got to make a shift to the stations further out;
The packhorse runs behind us, for he follows like a dog,
And we cross a lot of country at the old jig-jog.

THE TWO DEVINES

It was shearing-time at Myall Lake,
  And there rose the sound thro' the livelong day
Of the constant clash that the shear-blades make
  When the fastest shearers are making play,
But there wasn't a man in the shearers' lines
That could shear a sheep with the two Devines.

They had rung the sheds of the east and west,
  Had beaten the cracks of the Walgett side,
And the Cooma shearers had giv'n them best—
  When they saw them shear, they were satisfied.
From the southern slopes to the western pines
They were noted men, were the two Devines.

'Twas a wether flock that had come to hand,
  Great struggling brutes, that the shearers shirk,
For the fleece was filled with the grass and sand,
  And seventy sheep was a big day's work.
"At a pound a hundred it's dashed hard lines
To shear such sheep," said the two Devines.

But the shearers knew that they'd make a cheque
  When they came to deal with the station ewes;
They were bare of belly and bare of neck
  With a fleece as light as a kangaroo's.
"We will show the boss how a shear-blade shines
When we reach those ewes," said the two Devines.

But it chanced next day when the stunted pines
  Were swayed and stirred with the dawn-wind's breath,
That a message came for the two Devines
  That their father lay at the point of death.
So away at speed through the whispering pines
Down the bridle track rode the two Devines.

It was fifty miles to their father's hut,
  And the dawn was bright when they rode away;
At the fall of night when the shed was shut
  And the men had rest from the toilsome day,
To the shed once more through the dark'ning pines
On their weary steeds came the two Devines.

"Well you're back right sudden," the super. said;
  "Is the old man dead and the funeral done?"
"Well, no, sir, he ain't not exactly dead,
  But as good as dead," said the eldest son—
"And we couldn't bear such a chance to lose,
So we came straight back to tackle the ewes."

*   *   *

They are shearing ewes at the Myall Lake,
  And the shed is merry the livelong day
With the clashing sound that the shear-blades make
  When the fastest shearers are making play,
And a couple of "hundred and ninety-nines"
Are the tallies made by the two Devines.

THE GEEBUNG POLO CLUB

It was somewhere up the country, in a land of rock and scrub,
That they formed an institution called the Geebung Polo Club.
They were long and wiry natives from the rugged mountain side,
And the horse was never saddled that the Geebungs couldn't ride;
But their style of playing polo was irregular and rash—
They had mighty little science, but a mighty lot of dash:
And they played on mountain ponies that were muscular and strong,
Though their coats were quite unpolished, and their manes and tails
    were long.
And they used to train those ponies wheeling cattle in the scrub:
They were demons, were the members of the Geebung Polo Club.

It was somewhere down the country, in a city's smoke and steam,
That the polo club existed, called "The Cuff and Collar Team".
As a social institution 'twas a marvellous success,
For the members were distinguished by exclusiveness and dress.
They had natty little ponies that were nice, and smooth, and sleek,
For their cultivated owners only rode 'em once a week.
So they started up the country in pursuit of sport and fame,
For they meant to show the Geebungs how they ought to play the game;
And they took their valets with them—just to give their boots a rub
Ere they started operations on the Geebung Polo Club.

Now my readers can imagine how the contest ebbed and flowed,
When the Geebung boys got going it was time to clear the road;

And the game was so terrific that ere half the time was gone
A spectator's leg was broken—just from merely looking on.
For they waddied one another till the plain was strewn with dead,
While the score was kept so even that they neither got ahead.
And the Cuff and Collar Captain, when he tumbled off to die,
Was the last surviving player—so the game was called a tie.

Then the Captain of the Geebungs raised him slowly from the ground,
Though his wounds were mostly mortal, yet he fiercely gazed around;
There was no one to oppose him—all the rest were in a trance,
So he scrambled on his pony for his last expiring chance,
For he meant to make an effort to get victory to his side;
So he struck at goal—and missed it—then he tumbled off and died.

By the old Campaspe River, where the breezes shake the grass,
There's a row of little gravestones that the stockmen never pass,
For they bear a crude inscription saying, "Stranger, drop a tear,
For the Cuff and Collar players and the Geebung boys lie here."
And on misty moonlit evenings, while the dingoes howl around,
You can see their shadows flitting down that phantom polo ground;
You can hear the loud collisions as the flying players meet,
And the rattle of the mallets, and the rush of ponies' feet,
Till the terrified spectator rides like blazes to the pub—
He's been haunted by the spectres of the Geebung Polo Club.

MULGA BILL'S BICYCLE

'Twas Mulga Bill, from Eaglehawk, that caught the cycling craze;
He turned away the good old horse that served him many days;
He dressed himself in cycling clothes, resplendent to be seen;
He hurried off to town and bought a shining new machine;
And as he wheeled it through the door, with air of lordly pride,
The grinning shop assistant said, "Excuse me, can you ride?"

"See, here, young man," said Mulga Bill, "from Walgett to the sea,
From Conroy's Gap to Castlereagh, there's none can ride like me.
I'm good all round at everything, as everybody knows,
Although I'm not the one to talk—I *hate* a man that blows.
But riding is my special gift, my chiefest, sole delight;
Just ask a wild duck can it swim, a wild cat can it fight.
There's nothing clothed in hair or hide, or built of flesh or steel,
There's nothing walks or jumps, or runs, on axle, hoof, or wheel,
But what I'll sit, while hide will hold and girths and straps are tight:
I'll ride this here two-wheeled concern right straight away at sight."

'Twas Mulga Bill, from Eaglehawk, that sought his own abode,
That perched above the Dead Man's Creek, beside the mountain road.
He turned the cycle down the hill and mounted for the fray,
But ere he'd gone a dozen yards it bolted clean away.
It left the track, and through the trees, just like a silver streak,
It whistled down the awful slope, towards the Dead Man's Creek.

It shaved a stump by half an inch, it dodged a big white-box:
The very wallaroos in fright went scrambling up the rocks,
The wombats hiding in their caves dug deeper underground,
As Mulga Bill, as white as chalk, sat tight to every bound.
It struck a stone and gave a spring that cleared a fallen tree,
It raced beside a precipice as close as close could be;
And then as Mulga Bill let out one last despairing shriek
It made a leap of twenty feet into the Dead Man's Creek.

'Twas Mulga Bill, from Eaglehawk, that slowly swam ashore:
He said, "I've had some narrer shaves and lively rides before;
I've rode a wild bull round a yard to win a five pound bet,
But this was the most awful ride that I've encountered yet.
I'll give that two-wheeled outlaw best; it's shaken all my nerve
To feel it whistle through the air and plunge and buck and swerve.
It's safe at rest in Dead Man's Creek, we'll leave it lying still;
A horse's back is good enough henceforth for Mulga Bill."

JIM CAREW

Born of a thoroughbred English race,
    Well proportioned and closely knit,
Neat of figure and handsome face,
    Always ready and always fit,
Hard and wiry of limb and thew,
That was the ne'er-do-well Jim Carew.

One of the sons of the good old land—
    Many a year since his like was known;
Never a game but he took command,
    Never a sport but he held his own;
Gained at his college a triple blue—
Good as they make them was Jim Carew.

Came to grief—was it card or horse?
    Nobody asked and nobody cared;
Ship him away to the bush of course,
    Ne'er-do-well fellows are easily spared;
Only of women a tolerable few
Sorrowed at parting with Jim Carew.

Gentleman Jim on the cattle camp,
    Sitting his horse with an easy grace;
But the reckless living has left its stamp
    In the deep drawn lines of that handsome face,
And a harder look in those eyes of blue:
Prompt at a quarrel is Jim Carew.

Billy the Lasher was out for gore—
    Twelve-stone navvy with chest of hair,
When he opened out with a hungry roar
    On a ten-stone man it was hardly fair;
But his wife was wise if his face she knew
By the time you were done with him, Jim Carew.

Gentleman Jim in the stockmen's hut
    Works with them, toils with them, side by side;
As to his past—well, his lips are shut,
"Gentleman once," say his mates with pride,
And the wildest Cornstalk can ne'er outdo
In feats of recklessness, Jim Carew.

What should he live for? A dull despair!
    Drink is his master and drags him down,
Water of Lethe that drowns all care.
    Gentleman Jim has a lot to drown,
And he reigns as king with a drunken crew,
Sinking to misery, Jim Carew.

Such is the end of the ne'er-do-well—
    Jimmy the Boozer, all down at heel;
But he straightens up when he's asked to tell
    His name and race, and a flash of steel
Still lightens up in those eyes of blue—
"I am, or—no I *was*—Jim Carew."

How M'Ginnis Went Missing

Let us cease our idle chatter,
  Let the tears bedew our cheek,
For a man from Tallangatta
  Has been missing for a week.

Where the roaring flooded Murray
  Covered all the lower land,
There he started in a hurry,
  With a bottle in his hand.

And his fate is hid for ever,
  But the public seem to think
That he slumbered by the river,
  'Neath the influence of drink.

And they scarcely seem to wonder
  That the river, wide and deep,
Never woke him with its thunder,
  Never stirred him in his sleep.

As the crashing logs came sweeping,
  And their tumult filled the air,
Then M'Ginnis murmured, sleeping,
  " 'Tis a wake in ould Kildare."

So the river rose and found him
  Sleeping softly by the stream,
And the cruel waters drowned him
  Ere he wakened from his dream.

And the blossom-tufted wattle,
  Blooming brightly on the lea,
Saw M'Ginnis and the bottle
  Going drifting out to sea.

WALTZING MATILDA

Once a jolly swagman camped by a billabong,
  Under the shade of a coolibah tree,
And he sang as he watched and waited 'til his billy boiled,
  "Who'll come a-waltzing Matilda with me—
 Waltzing Matilda, waltzing Matilda, who'll come a-waltzing
  Matilda with me?"
And he sang as he watched and waited 'til his billy boiled,
  "Who'll come a-waltzing Matilda with me?"

Down came a jumbuck to drink at the billabong
  Up jumped the swagman and grabbed him with glee,
And he sang, as he stowed that jumbuck in his tucker-bag,
  "Who'll come a-waltzing Matilda with me?
Waltzing Matilda, waltzing Matilda, who'll come a-waltzing
  Matilda with me?"
And he sang as he stowed that jumbuck in his tucker-bag,
  "Who'll come a-waltzing Matilda with me?"

Up came the squatter, mounted on his thoroughbred,
  Down came the troopers—one, two, three—
"Whose is the jolly jumbuck, you've got in your tucker-bag?
  You'll come a-waltzing Matilda with me.
Waltzing Matilda, waltzing Matilda, who'll come a-waltzing
  Matilda with me?
Whose is the jolly jumbuck you've got in your tucker-bag.
  You'll come a-waltzing Matilda with me."

Up jumped the swagman, and sprang into the billabong,
  "You'll never take me alive!" said he.
And his ghost may be heard, as we pass by that billabong,
  "Who'll come a-waltzing Matilda with me?
Waltzing Matilda, waltzing Matilda,
  Who'll come a-waltzing Matilda with me?"
And his ghost may be heard, as we pass by that billabong,
  "Who'll come a-waltzing Matilda with me?"

HAY AND HELL AND BOOLIGAL

"You come and see me, boys," he said;
"You'll find a welcome and a bed
   And whisky any time you call;
Although our township hasn't got
The name of quite a lively spot—
   You see, I live in Booligal.

"And people have an awful down
Upon the district and the town—
   Which worse than hell itself they call;
In fact, the saying far and wide
Along the Riverina side
   Is "Hay and Hell and Booligal".

"No doubt it suits 'em very well
To say it's worse than Hay or Hell,
   But don't you heed their talk at all;
Of course, there's heat—no one denies—
And sand and dust and stacks of flies,
   And rabbits, too, at Booligal.

"But such a pleasant, quiet place,
You never see a stranger's face—
   They hardly ever care to call;
The drovers mostly pass it by;
They reckon that they'd rather die
   Than spend a night in Booligal.

"The big mosquitoes frighten some—
You'll lie awake to hear 'em hum—
   And snakes about the township crawl;
But shearers, when they get their cheque,
They never come along and wreck
   The blessed town of Booligal.

"But down in Hay the shearers come
And fill themselves with fighting rum,
   And chase blue devils up the wall,
And fight the snaggers every day,
Until there is the deuce to pay—
   There's none of that in Booligal.

"Of course, there isn't much to see—
The billiard table used to be
   The great attraction for us all,
Until some careless, drunken curs
Got sleeping on it in their spurs,
   And ruined it, in Booligal.

"Just now there is a howling drought
That pretty near has starved us out—
   It never seems to rain at all;
But, if there *should* come any rain,
You couldn't cross the black soil plain—
   You'd have to stop in Booligal."

"We'd have to stop!" With bated breath
We prayed that both in life and death
   Our fate in other lines might fall:
"Oh, send us to our just reward
In Hay or Hell, but, gracious Lord,
   Deliver us from Booligal!"

BLACK SWANS

As I lie at rest on a patch of clover
In the Western Park when the day is done,
I watch as the wild black swans fly over
With their phalanx turned to the sinking sun;
And I hear the clang of their leader crying
To a lagging mate in the rearward flying,
And they fade away in the darkness dying,
Where the stars are mustering one by one.

Oh! ye wild black swans, 'twere a world of wonder
For a while to join in your westward flight,
With the stars above and the dim earth under,
Through the cooling air of the glorious night.
As we swept along on our pinions winging,
We should catch the chime of a church-bell ringing,
Or the distant note of a torrent singing,
Or the far-off flash of a station light.

From the northern lakes with the reeds and rushes,
Where the hills are clothed with purple haze,
Where the bell-birds chime and the songs of thrushes
Make music sweet in the jungle maze,
They will hold their course to the westward ever,
Till they reach the banks of the old grey river,
Where the waters wash, and the reed-beds quiver
In the burning heat of the summer days.

Oh! ye strange wild birds, will ye bear a greeting
To the folk that live in that western land?
Then for every sweep of your pinions beating,
Ye shall bear a wish to the sunburnt band,
To the stalwart men who are stoutly fighting
With the heat and drought and the dust-storm smiting,
Yet whose life somehow has a strange inviting,
When once to the work they have put their hand.

Facing it yet! Oh, my friend stout-hearted,
What does it matter for rain or shine,
For the hopes deferred and the gain departed?
Nothing could conquer that heart of thine.
And thy health and strength are beyond confessing
As the only joys that are worth possessing.
May the days to come be as rich in blessing
As the days we spent in the auld lang syne.

I would fain go back to the old grey river,
To the old bush days when our hearts were light,
But, alas! those days they have fled for ever,
They are like the swans that have swept from sight.
And I know full well that the strangers' faces
Would meet us now in our dearest places;
For our day is dead and has left no traces
But the thoughts that live in my mind to-night.

There are folk long dead, and our hearts would sicken—
We would grieve for them with a bitter pain,
If the past could live and the dead could quicken,
We then might turn to that life again.
But on lonely nights we would hear them calling,
We should hear their steps on the pathways falling,
We should loathe the life with a hate appalling
In our lonely rides by the ridge and plain.

*   *   *

In the silent park is a scent of clover,
And the distant roar of the town is dead,
And I hear once more as the swans fly over
Their far-off clamour from overhead.
They are flying west, by their instinct guided,
And for man likewise is his fate decided,
And griefs apportioned and joys divided
By a mighty power with a purpose dread.

CLANCY OF THE OVERFLOW

I had written him a letter which I had, for want of better
    Knowledge, sent to where I met him down the Lachlan, years ago;
He was shearing when I knew him, so I sent the letter to him,
    Just "on spec", addressed as follows: "Clancy, of The Overflow".

And an answer came directed in a writing unexpected,
    (And I think the same was written with a thumbnail dipped in tar);
'Twas his shearing mate who wrote it, and *verbatim* I will quote it:
    "Clancy's gone to Queensland droving, and we don't know where he are."

* * *

In my wild erratic fancy visions come to me of Clancy
    Gone a-droving "down the Cooper" where the Western drovers go;
As the stock are slowly stringing, Clancy rides behind them singing,
    For the drover's life has pleasures that the townsfolk never know.

And the bush hath friends to meet him, and their kindly voices greet
    him
    In the murmur of the breezes and the river on its bars,
And he sees the vision splendid of the sunlit plains extended,
    And at night the wondrous glory of the everlasting stars.

* * *

I am sitting in my dingy little office, where a stingy
    Ray of sunlight struggles feebly down between the houses tall,
And the foetid air and gritty of the dusty, dirty city
    Through the open window floating, spreads its foulness over all.

And in place of lowing cattle, I can hear the fiendish rattle
    Of the tramways and the buses making hurry down the street,
And the language uninviting of the gutter children fighting,
    Comes fitfully and faintly through the ceaseless tramp of feet.

And the hurrying people daunt me, and their pallid faces haunt me
    As they shoulder one another in their rush and nervous haste,
With their eager eyes and greedy, and their stunted forms and weedy,
    For townsfolk have no time to grow, they have no time to waste.

And I somehow rather fancy that I'd like to change with Clancy,
    Like to take a turn at droving where the seasons come and go,
While he faced the round eternal of the cashbook and the journal—
    But I doubt he'd suit the office, Clancy, of "The Overflow".

THE DAYLIGHT IS DYING

The daylight is dying
   Away in the west,
The wild birds are flying
   In silence to rest;
In leafage and frondage
   Where shadows are deep,
They pass to its bondage—
   The kingdom of sleep.
And watched in their sleeping
   By stars in the height,
They rest in your keeping,
   Oh, wonderful night.

When night doth her glories
   Of starshine unfold,
'Tis then that the stories
   Of bushland are told.
Unnumbered I hold them
   In memories bright,
But who could unfold them,
   Or read them aright?

Beyond all denials
   The stars in their glories
The breeze in the myalls
   Are part of these stories.
The waving of grasses,
   The song of the river

That sings as it passes
   For ever and ever,
The hobble chains rattle,
   The calling of birds,
The lowing of cattle
   Must blend with the words.

Without these, indeed, you
   Would find it ere long,
As though I should read you
   The words of a song
That lamely would linger
   When lacking the rune,
The voice of the singer,
   The lilt of the tune.

But, as one half-hearing
   An old-time refrain,
With memory clearing,
   Recalls it again,
These tales, roughly wrought of
   The bush and its ways,
May call back a thought of
   The wandering days,
And, blending with each
   In the mem'ries that throng,
There haply shall reach
   You some echo of song.

SALTBUSH BILL'S SECOND FIGHT

The news came down on the Castlereagh, and went to the world at large,
That twenty thousand travelling sheep, with Saltbush Bill in charge,
Were drifting down from a dried-out run to ravage the Castlereagh;
And the squatters swore when they heard the news, and wished they were well away:
For the name and the fame of Saltbush Bill were over the country side
For the wonderful way that he fed his sheep, and the dodges and tricks he tried.
He would lose his way on a Main Stock Route, and stray to the squatters' grass;
He would come to the run with the boss away, and swear he had leave to pass;
And back of all and behind it all, as well the squatters knew,
If he had to fight, he would fight all day, so long as his sheep got through:
But this is the story of Stingy Smith, the owner of Hard Times Hill,
And the way that he chanced on a fighting man to reckon with Saltbush Bill.

*   *   *

'Twas Stingy Smith on his stockyard sat, and prayed for an early Spring,
When he stared at sight of a clean-shaved tramp, who walked with a jaunty swing;
For a clean-shaved tramp with a jaunty walk a-swinging along the track
Is as rare a thing as a feathered frog on the desolate roads out back.
So the tramp he made for the travellers' hut, and asked could he camp the night;
But Stingy Smith had a bright idea, and he said to him, "Can you fight?"
"Why, what's the game?" said the clean-shaved tramp, as he looked at him up and down—
"If you want a battle, get off that fence, and I'll kill you for half-a-crown!
But, Boss, you'd better not fight with me, it wouldn't be fair nor right;
I'm Stiffener Joe, from the Rocks Brigade, and I killed a man in a fight:
I served two years for it, fair and square, and now I'm a trampin' back,
To look for a peaceful quiet life away on the outside track—"
"Oh, it's not myself, but a drover chap," said Stingy Smith with glee;
"A bullying fellow, called Saltbush Bill—and you are the man for me.
He's on the road with his hungry sheep, and he's certain to raise a row,
For he's bullied the whole of the Castlereagh till he's got them under cow—
Just pick a quarrel and raise a fight, and leather him good and hard,
And I'll take good care that his wretched sheep don't wander half a yard.

It's a five-pound job if you belt him well—do anything short of kill,
For there isn't a beak on the Castlereagh will fine you for Saltbush Bill."

"I'll take the job," said the fighting man; "and hot as this cove appears,
He'll stand no chance with a bloke like me, what's lived on the game for years;
For he's maybe learnt in a boxing school, and sparred for a round or so,
But I've fought all hands in a ten-foot ring each night in a travelling show;
They earned a pound if they stayed three rounds, and they tried for it every night—
In a ten-foot ring! Oh, that's the game that teaches a bloke to fight,
For they'd rush and clinch, it was Dublin Rules, and we drew no colour line;
And they all tried hard for to earn the pound, but they got no pound of mine:
If I saw no chance in the opening round I'd slog at their wind, and wait
Till an opening came—and it *always* came—and I settled 'em, sure as fate;
Left on the ribs and right on the jaw—and, when the chance comes, *make sure!*
And it's there a professional bloke like me gets home on an amateur:
For it's my experience every day. and I make no doubt it's yours,
That a third-class pro is an over-match for the best of the amateurs—"

"Oh, take your swag to the travellers' hut," said Smith, "for you waste your breath;
You've a first-class chance, if you lose the fight, of talking your man to death.
I'll tell the cook you're to have your grub, and see that you eat your fill,
And come to the scratch all fit and well to leather this Saltbush Bill."

*   *   *

'Twas Saltbush Bill, and his travelling sheep were wending their weary way
On the Main Stock Route, through the Hard Times Run, on their six-mile stage a day;
And he strayed a mile from the Main Stock Route, and started to feed along,
And, when Stingy Smith came up, Bill said that the Route was surveyed wrong;
And he tried to prove that the sheep had rushed and strayed from their camp at night,
But the fighting man he kicked Bill's dog, and of course that meant a fight:
So they sparred and fought, and they shifted ground, and never a sound was heard
But the thudding fists on their brawny ribs, and the seconds' muttered word,
Till the fighting man shot home his left on the ribs with a mighty clout,
And his right flashed up with a half-arm blow—and Saltbush Bill "went out".
He fell face down, and towards the blow; and their hearts with fear were filled,
For he lay as still as a fallen tree, and they thought that he must be killed.

So Stingy Smith and the fighting man, they lifted him from the ground,
And sent to home for a brandy flask, and they slowly fetched him round;
But his head was bad, and his jaw was hurt—in fact, he could scarcely speak—
So they let him spell till he got his wits, and he camped on the run for a week,
While the travelling sheep went here and there, wherever they liked to stray,
Till Saltbush Bill was fit once more for the track to the Castlereagh.

Then Stingy Smith he wrote a note, and gave to the fighting man:
'Twas writ to the boss of the neighbouring run, and thus the missive ran:
"The man with this is a fighting man, one Stiffener Joe by name;
He came near murdering Saltbush Bill, and I found it a costly game:
But it's worth your while to employ the chap, for there isn't the slightest doubt
You'll have no trouble from Saltbush Bill while this man hangs about—"
But an answer came by the next week's mail, with news that might well appal:
"The man you sent with a note is not a fighting man at all!
He has shaved his beard, and has cut his hair, but I spotted him at a look;
He is Tom Devine, who has worked for years for Saltbush Bill as cook.
Bill coached him up in the fighting yarn, and taught him the tale by rote,
And they shammed to fight, and they got your grass and divided your five-pound note.
'Twas a clean take-in, and you'll find it wise—'twill save you a lot of pelf—
When next you're hiring a fighting man, just fight him a round yourself."

And the teamsters out on the Castlereagh, when they meet with a week of rain,
And the waggon sinks to its axle-tree, deep down in the black soil plain,
When the bullocks wade in a sea of mud, and strain at the load of wool,
And the cattle dogs at the bullocks' heels are biting to make them pull,
When the offside driver flays the team, and curses them while he flogs,
And the air is thick with the language used, and the clamour of men and dogs—
The teamsters say, as they pause to rest and moisten each hairy throat,
They wish they could swear like Stingy Smith when he read that neighbour's note.

THE ROAD TO GUNDAGAI

The mountain road goes up and down,
From Gundagai to Tumut town.

And branching off there runs a track,
Across the foothills grim and black,

Across the plains and ranges grey
To Sydney city far away.

It came by chance one day that I
From Tumut rode to Gundagai.

And reached about the evening tide
The crossing where the roads divide;

And, waiting at the crossing place,
I saw a maiden fair of face,

With eyes of deepest violet blue,
And cheeks to match the rose in hue—

The fairest maids Australia knows
Are bred among the mountain snows.

Then, fearing I might go astray,
I asked if she could show the way.

Her voice might well a man bewitch—
Its tones so supple, deep, and rich.

"The tracks are clear," she made reply,
"And this goes down to Sydney town,
And that one goes to Gundagai."

Then slowly, looking coyly back,
She went along the Sydney track.

And I for one was well content
To go the road the lady went;

But round the turn a swain she met—
The kiss she gave him haunts me yet!

I turned and travelled with a sigh
The lonely road to Gundagai.

BRUMBY'S RUN

Brumby is the Aboriginal word for a wild horse.
*   At a recent trial a New South Wales Supreme*
Court Judge, hearing of Brumby horses, asked:
"Who is Brumby, and where is his run?"

It lies beyond the Western Pines
    Beneath the sinking sun,
And not a survey mark defines
    The bounds of 'Brumby's Run'.

On odds and ends of mountain land,
    On tracks of range and rock
Where no one else can make a stand
    Old Brumby rears his stock.

A wild, unhandled lot they are
    Of every shape and breed.
They venture out neath moon and star
    Along the flats to feed;

But, when the dawn makes pink the sky
    And steals along the plain,
The Brumby horses turn and fly
    Back to the hills again.

The traveller by the mountain-track
    May hear their hoof-beats pass,
And catch a glimpse of brown and black
    Dim shadows on the grass.

The eager stockhorse pricks his ears,
    And lifts his head on high
In wild excitement, when he hears
    The Brumby mob go by.

Old Brumby asks no price or fee
    O'er all his wide domains:
The man who yards his stock is free
    To keep them for his pains.

So off to scour the mountain-side
    With eager eyes aglow,
To strongholds where the wild mobs hide
    The gully-rakers go.

A rush of horses through the trees,
    A red shirt making play;
A sound of stockwhips on the breeze,
    They vanish far away!

        *   *   *

Ah! me! before our day is done
    We long with bitter pain
To ride once more on Brumby's Run
    And yard his mob again.

THE SWAGMAN'S REST

We buried old Bob where the bloodwoods wave
  At the foot of the Eaglehawk;
We fashioned a cross on the old man's grave,
  For fear that his ghost might walk;
We carved his name on a bloodwood tree,
  With the date of his sad decease,
And in place of "Died from effects of spree",
  We wrote "May he rest in peace".

For Bob was known on the Overland,
  A regular old bush wag,
Tramping along in the dust and sand,
  Humping his well-worn swag.
He would camp for days in the river-bed,
  And loiter and "fish for whales".
"I'm into the swagman's yard," he said,
  "And I never shall find the rails."

But he found the rails on that summer night
  For a better place—or worse,
As we watched by turns in the flickering light
  With an old black gin for nurse.
The breeze came in with the scent of pine,
  The river sounded clear,
When a change came on, and we saw the sign
  That told us the end was near.

But he spoke in a cultured voice and low—
  "I fancy they've 'sent the route';
I once was an army man, you know,
  Though now I'm a drunken brute;
But bury me out where the bloodwoods wave,

And if ever you're fairly stuck,
Just take and shovel me out of the grave
  And, maybe, I'll bring you luck.

"For I've always heard—" here his voice fell weak,
  His strength was well-nigh sped,
He gasped and struggled and tried to speak,
  Then fell in a moment—dead.
Thus ended a wasted life and hard,
  Of energies misapplied—
Old Bob was out of the "swagman's yard"
  And over the Great Divide.

 *   *   *

The drought came down on the field and flock,
  And never a raindrop fell,
Though the tortured moans of the starving stock
  Might soften a fiend from hell.
And we thought of the hint that the swagman gave
  When he went to the Great Unseen—
We shovelled the skeleton out of the grave
  To see what his hint might mean.

We dug where the cross and the grave posts were,
  We shovelled away the mould,
When sudden a vein of quartz lay bare
  All gleaming with yellow gold.
'Twas a reef with never a fault nor baulk
  That ran from the range's crest,
And the richest mine on the Eaglehawk
  Is known as "The Swagman's Rest".

SALTBUSH BILL'S GAMECOCK

'Twas Saltbush Bill, with his travelling sheep, was making his way to town;
He crossed them over the Hard Times Run, and he came to the Take 'Em Down;
He counted through at the boundary gate, and camped at the drafting yard:
For Stingy Smith, of the Hard Times Run, had hunted him rather hard.
He bore no malice to Stingy Smith—'twas simply the hand of fate
That caused his waggon to swerve aside and shatter old Stingy's gate;
And, being only the hand of fate, it follows, without a doubt,
It wasn't the fault of Saltbush Bill that Stingy's sheep got out.
So, Saltbush Bill, with an easy heart, prepared for what might befall,
Commenced his stages on Take 'Em Down, the station of Rooster Hall.

'Tis strange how often the men out back will take to some curious craft,
Some ruling passion to keep their thoughts away from the overdraft;
And Rooster Hall, of the Take 'Em Down, was widely known to fame
As breeder of champion fighting cocks—his *forte* was the British Game.
The passing stranger within his gates that camped with old Rooster Hall
Was forced to talk about fowls all night, or else not talk at all.
Through droughts should come, and though sheep should die, his fowls were his sole delight;

He left his shed in the flood of work to watch two gamecocks fight.
He held in scorn the Australian Game, that long-legged child of sin;
In a desperate fight, with the steel-tipped spurs, the British Game must win!
The Australian bird was a mongrel bird, with a touch of the jungle cock;
The want of breeding must find him out, when facing the English stock;
For British breeding, and British pluck, must triumph it over all—
And that was the root of the simple creed that governed old Rooster Hall.

*   *   *

'Twas Saltbush Bill to the station rode ahead of his travelling sheep,
And sent a message to Rooster Hall that wakened him out of his sleep—
A crafty message that fetched him out, and hurried him as he came—
"A drover has an Australian bird to match with your British Game."
'Twas done, and done in half a trice; a five-pound note aside;
Old Rooster Hall, with his champion bird, and the drover's bird untried.
"Steel spurs, of course?" said old Rooster Hall; "you'll need 'em, without a doubt!"
"You stick the spurs on your bird," said Bill! "but mine fights best without."
"Fights best without?" said old Rooster Hall; "he can't fight best unspurred!
You must be crazy!" But Saltbush Bill said, "Wait till you see my bird!"
So Rooster Hall to his fowlyard went, and quickly back he came,
Bearing a clipt and a shaven cock, the pride of his English Game.
With an eye as fierce as an eaglehawk, and a crow like a trumpet call,
He strutted about on the garden walk, and cackled at Rooster Hall.
Then Rooster Hall sent off a boy with word to his cronies two,
McCrae (the boss of the Black Police) and Father Donahoo.
Full many a cockfight old McCrae had held in his empty Court,
With Father D. as a picker-up—a regular all-round Sport!
They got the message of Rooster Hall, and down to his run they came,
Prepared to scoff at the drover's bird, and to bet on the English Game;
They hied them off to the drover's camp, while Saltbush rode before—
Old Rooster Hall was a blithesome man, when he thought of the treat in store.
They reached the camp, where the drover's cook, with countenance all serene,
Was boiling beef in an iron pot, but never a fowl was seen.

"Take off the beef from the fire," said Bill, "and wait till you see the fight;
There's something fresh for the bill-of-fare—there's game-fowl stew to-night!
For Mister Hall has a fighting cock, all feathered and clipped and spurred;
And he's fetched him here, for a bit of sport, to fight our Australian bird.
I've made a match that our pet will win, though he's hardly a fighting cock,
But he's game enough, and it's many a mile that he's tramped with the travelling stock."
The cook he banged on a saucepan lid; and, soon as the sound was heard,
Under the dray, in the shadows hid, a something moved and stirred:
A great tame Emu strutted out. Said Saltbush, "Here's our bird!"
But Rooster Hall, and his cronies two, drove home without a word.

The passing stranger within his gates that camps with old Rooster Hall
Must talk about something else than fowls, if he wishes to talk at all.
For the record lies in the local Court, and filed in its deepest vault,
That Peter Hall, of the Take 'Em Down, was tried for a fierce assault
On a stranger man, who, in all good faith, and prompted by what he heard,
Had asked old Hall if a British Game could beat an Australian bird;
And old McCrae, who was on the Bench, as soon as the case was tried,
Remarked, "Discharged with a clean discharge—the assault was justified!"

THE STORY OF MONGREL GREY

This is the story the stockman told,
On the cattle camp, when the stars were bright;
The moon rose up like a globe of gold
And flooded the plain with her mellow light.
We watched the cattle till dawn of day
And he told me the story of Mongrel Grey.

"He was a knock-about station hack,
Spurred and walloped, and banged and beat;
Ridden all day with a sore on his back,
Left all night with nothing to eat.
That was a matter of everyday—
Common occurrence for Mongrel Grey.

"Pr'aps we'd have sold him, but someone heard
He was bred out back on a flooded run,
Where he learned to swim like a water bird,
Midnight or midday were all as one.
In the flooded ground he could find his way,
Nothing could puzzle old Mongrel Grey.

" 'Tis a special gift that some horses learn,
When the floods are out they will splash along
In girth-deep water, and twist and turn
From hidden channel and billabong.
Never mistaking the road to go,
For a man may guess—but the horses *know*.

"I was camping out with my youngest son
—Bit of a nipper just learnt to speak—
In an empty hut on the lower run,
Shooting and fishing in Conroy's Creek.
The youngster toddled about all day,
And with our horses was Mongrel Grey.

"All of a sudden the flood came down
Fresh from the hills with the mountain rain,
Roaring and eddying, rank and brown,
Over the flats and across the plain.
Rising and falling—fall of night—
Nothing but water appeared in sight!

" 'Tis a nasty place when the floods are out,
Even in daylight, for all around
Channels and billabongs twist about,
Stretching for miles in the flooded ground.
And to move was a hopeless thing to try
In the dark, with the water just racing by.

"I had to try it. I heard a roar,
And the wind swept down with the blinding rain;
And the water rose till it reached the floor
Of our highest room, and 'twas very plain
The way the water was sweeping down
We must shift for the highlands at once, or drown.

"Off to the stable I splashed, and found
The horses shaking with cold and fright;
I led them down to the lower ground,
But never a yard they swam that night!
They reared and snorted and turned away,
And none would face it but Mongrel Grey.

"I bound the child on the horse's back,
And we started off with a prayer to heaven,
Through the rain and wind and the pitchy black,
For I knew that the instinct God has given
To guide His creatures by night and day
Would lead the footsteps of Mongrel Grey.

"He struck deep water at once and swam—
I swam beside him and held his mane—
Till we touched the bank of the broken dam
In shallow water—then off again,
Swimming in darkness across the flood,
Rank with the smell of the drifting mud.

"He turned and twisted across and back,
Choosing the places to wade and swim,
Picking the safest and shortest track,
The pitchy darkness was clear to him.
Did he strike the crossing by sight or smell?
The Lord that led him alone could tell!

"He dodged the timber whene'er he could,
But the timber brought us to grief at last;
I was partly stunned by a log of wood,
That struck my head as it drifted past;
And I lost my grip of the brave old grey,
And in half a second he swept away.

"I reached a tree, where I had to stay,
And did a perish for two days hard;
And lived on water—but Mongrel Grey,
He walked right into the homestead yard
At dawn next morning, and grazed around,
With the child on top of him safe and sound.

"We keep him now for the wife to ride,
Nothing too good for him now of course;
Never a whip on his fat old hide,
For she owes the child to that old grey horse.
And not Old Tyson himself could pay,
The purchase money of Mongrel Grey."

AN EVENING IN DANDALOO

It was while we held our races—
Hurdles, sprints and steeplechases—
   Up in Dandaloo,
That a crowd of Sydney stealers,
Jockeys, pugilists and spielers
Brought some horses, real heelers,
   Came and put us through.

Beat our nags and won our money,
Made the game by no means funny,
   Made us rather blue;
When the racing was concluded,
Of our hard-earned coin denuded
Dandaloonies sat and brooded
   There in Dandaloo.

Night came down on Johnson's shanty
Where the grog was no way scanty,
   And a tumult grew
Till some wild, excited person
Galloped down the township cursing,
"Sydney push have mobbed Macpherson,
   Roll up, Dandaloo!"

Great St Denis! what commotion!
Like the rush of stormy ocean
   Fiery horsemen flew.
Dust and smoke and din and rattle,
Down the street they spurred their cattle
To the war-cry of the battle,
   "Wade in, Dandaloo!"

So the boys might have their fight out,
Johnson blew the bar-room light out,
   Then, in haste, withdrew.
And in darkness and in doubting
Raged the conflict and the shouting,
"Give the Sydney push a clouting,
   Go it, Dandaloo!"

Jack Macpherson seized a bucket,
Every head he saw he struck it—
   Struck in earnest, too;
And a man from Lower Wattle,
Whom a shearer tried to throttle,
Hit out freely with a bottle
   There in Dandaloo.

Skin and hair were flying thickly,
When a light was fetched, and quickly
   Brought a fact to view—
On the scene of the diversion
Every single, solid person
Come along to help Macpherson—
   All were Dandaloo!

When the list of slain was tabled—
Some were drunk and some disabled—
   Still we found it true.
In the darkness and the smother
We'd been belting one another;
Jack Macpherson bashed his brother
   There in Dandaloo.

So we drank, and all departed—
How the "mobbing" yarn was started
   No one ever knew—
And the stockmen tell the story
Of that conflict fierce and gory,
How we fought for love and glory
   Up in Dandaloo.

It's a proverb now, or near it—
At the races you can hear it,
   At the dog-fights, too!
Every shrieking, dancing drover
As the canines topple over
Yells applause to Grip or Rover,
   "Give him 'Dandaloo'!"

And the teamster slowly toiling
Through the deep black country, soiling
   Wheels and axles, too,
Lays the whip on Spot and Banker,
Rouses Tarboy with a flanker—
"Redman! Ginger! Heave there! Yank her!
   Wade in, Dandaloo!"

A BUSH CHRISTENING

On the outer Barcoo where the churches are few
    And men of religion are scanty,
On a road never cross'd 'cept by folk that are lost,
    One Michael Magee had a shanty.

Now this Mike was the dad of a ten year old lad,
    Plump, healthy, and stoutly conditioned;
He was strong as the best, but poor Mike had no rest
    For the youngster had never been christened.

And his wife used to cry, "If the darlin' should die
    Saint Peter would not recognise him."
But by luck he survived till a preacher arrived,
    Who agreed straightaway to baptise him.

Now the artful young rogue, while they held their collogue,
    With his ear to the keyhole was listenin',
And he muttered in fright, while his features turned white,
    "What the divil and all is this christenin'?"

He was none of your dolts, he had seen them brand colts,
    And it seemed to his small understanding,
If the man in the frock made him one of the flock,
    It must mean something very like branding.

So away with a rush he set off for the bush,
    While the tears in his eyelids they glistened—
" 'Tis outrageous," says he, "to brand youngsters like me,
    I'll be dashed if I'll stop to be christened!"

Like a young native dog he ran into a log,
    And his father with language uncivil,
Never heeding the 'praste' cried aloud in his haste,
    "Come out and be christened, you divil!"

But he lay there as snug as a bug in a rug,
    And his parents in vain might reprove him,
Till his reverence spoke (he was fond of a joke)
    "I've a notion," says he, "that'll move him.

"Poke a stick up the log, give the spalpeen a prog;
    Poke him aisy—don't hurt him or maim him,
'Tis not long that he'll stand, I've the water at hand,
    As he rushes out this end I'll name him.

"Here he comes, and for shame! ye've forgotten the name—
    Is it Patsy of Michael or Dinnis?"
Here the youngster ran out, and the priest gave shout—
    "Take your chance, anyhow, wid 'Maginnis'!"

As the howling young cub ran away to the scrub
    Where he knew that pursuit would be risky,
The priest, as he fled, flung a flask at his head
    That was labelled *Maginnis's Whisky!*

And Maginnis Magee has been made a J.P.,
    And the one thing he hates more than sin is
To be asked by the folk, who have heard of the joke,
    How he came to be christened "Maginnis"!

THE TRAVELLING POST OFFICE

The roving breezes come and go, the reed beds sweep and sway,
The sleepy river murmurs low, and loiters on its way,
It is the land of lots o' time along the Castlereagh.

*　　　　*　　　　*

The old man's son had left the farm, he found it dull and slow,
He drifted to the great North-west where all the rovers go.
"He's gone so long," the old man said, "he's dropped right out of mind,
But if you'd write a line to him I'd take it very kind;
He's shearing here and fencing there, a kind of waif and stray,
He's droving now with Conroy's sheep along the Castlereagh.
The sheep are travelling for the grass, and travelling very slow;
They may be at Mundooran now, or past the Overflow,
Or tramping down the black soil flats across by Waddiwong,
But all those little country towns would send the letter wrong,
The mailman, if he's extra tired, would pass them in his sleep,
It's safest to address the note to 'Care of Conroy's sheep'.
For five and twenty thousand head can scarcely go astray,
You write to 'Care of Conroy's sheep along the Castlereagh'."

*　　　　*　　　　*

By rock and ridge and riverside the western mail has gone,
Across the great Blue Mountain Range to take that letter on.
A moment on the topmost grade while open fire doors glare,
She pauses like a living thing to breathe the mountain air,
Then launches down the other side across the plains away
To bear that note to "Conroy's sheep along the Castlereagh".
And now by coach and mailman's bag it goes from town to town,
And Conroy's Gap and Conroy's Creek have marked it "further down".
Beneath a sky of deepest blue where never cloud abides,
A speck upon the waste of plain the lonely mailman rides.
Where fierce hot winds have set the pine and myall boughs asweep
He hails the shearers passing by for news of Conroy's sheep.
By big lagoons where wildfowl play and crested pigeons flock,
By campfires where the drovers ride around their restless stock,
And pass the teamster toiling down to fetch the wool away
My letter chases Conroy's sheep along the Castlereagh.

PIONEERS

They came of bold and roving stock that would not fixed abide;
They were the sons of field and flock since e'er they learned to ride;
We may not hope to see such men in these degenerate years
As those explorers of the bush—the brave old pioneers.

'Twas they who rode the trackless bush in heat and storm and
     drought;
'Twas they that heard the master-word that called them further out;
'Twas they that followed up the trail the mountain cattle made
And pressed across the mighty range where now their bones are laid.

But now the times are dull and slow, the brave old days are dead
When hardy bushmen started out, and forced their way ahead
By tangled scrub and forests grim towards the unknown west,
And spied the far-off promised land from off the ranges' crest.

Oh! ye, that sleep in lonely graves by far-off ridge and plain,
We drink to you in silence now as Christmas comes again,
The men who fought the wilderness through rough, unsettled years—
The founders of our nation's life, the brave old pioneers.

BOTTLE-O!

I ain't the kind of bloke as takes to any steady job;
  I drives me bottle cart around the town;
A bloke what keeps 'is eyes about can always make a bob—
  I couldn't bear to graft for every brown.
There's lots of handy things about in everybody's yard,
  There's cocks and hens a-runnin' to an' fro,
And little dogs what comes and barks—we take 'em off their guard
  And we puts 'em with the Empty Bottle-O!

Chorus—
  So it's any "Empty bottles! Any empty bottle-O!"
  You can hear us round for half a mile or so.
    And you'll see the women rushing
    To take in the Monday's washing
  When they 'ear us crying, "Empty Bottle-O!"

I'm drivin' down by Wexford-street and up a winder goes,
  A girl sticks out 'er 'ead and looks at me,
An all-right tart with ginger 'air, and freckles on 'er nose;
  I stops the cart and walks across to see.
"There ain't no bottles 'ere," says she, "since father took the pledge;"
  "No bottles 'ere," says I, "I'd like to know
What right you 'ave to stick your 'ead outside the winder ledge,
  If you 'aven't got no Empty Bottle-O!"

I sometimes gives the 'orse a spell, and then the push and me
  We takes a little trip to Chowder Bay.
Oh! ain't it nice the 'ole day long a-gazin' at the sea
  And a-hidin' of the tanglefoot away.
But when the booze gits 'old of us, and fellows starts to "scrap",
  There's some what likes blue-metal for to throw:
But as for me, I always says for layin' out a "trap"
  There's nothing like an Empty Bottle-O!

58

OLD PARDON, THE SON OF REPRIEVE

You never heard tell of the story?
    Well, now, I can hardly believe!
Never heard of the honour and glory
    Of Pardon, the son of Reprieve?
But maybe you're only a Johnnie
    And don't know a horse from a hoe?
Well, well, don't get angry, my sonny,
    But, really, a young 'un should know.

They bred him out back on the "Never",
    His mother was Mameluke breed.
To the front—and then stay there—was ever
    The root of the Mameluke creed.
He seemed to inherit their wiry
    Strong frames—and their pluck to receive—
As hard as flint and as fiery
    Was Pardon, the son of Reprieve.

We ran him at many a meeting
    At crossing and gully and town,
And nothing could give him a beating—
    At least when our money was down.
For weight wouldn't stop him, nor distance,
    Nor odds, though the others were fast,
He'd race with a dogged persistence,
    And wear them all down at the last.

At the Turon the Yattendon filly
    Led by lengths at the mile-and-a-half,
And we all began to look silly,
    While *her* crowd were starting to laugh;
But the old horse came faster and faster,
    His pluck told its tale, and his strength,
He gained on her, caught her, and passed her,
    And won it, hands-down, by a length.

And then we swooped down on Menindie
    To run for the President's Cup—
Oh! that's a sweet township—a shindy
    To them is board, lodging, and sup.
Eye-openers they are, and their system
    Is never to suffer defeat;
It's "win, tie, or wrangle"—to best 'em
    You must lose 'em, or else it's "dead heat".

We strolled down the township and found 'em
    At drinking and gaming and play;
If sorrows they had, why they drowned 'em,
    And betting was soon under way.
Their horses were good 'uns and fit 'uns,
    There was plenty of cash in the town;
They backed their own horses like Britons,
    And, Lord! how *we* rattled it down!

With gladness we thought of the morrow,
    We counted our wagers with glee,
A simile homely to borrow—
    "There was plenty of milk in our tea."
You see we were green; and we never
    Had even a thought of foul play,

Though we well might have known that the clever
    Division would "put us away."

Experience *docet*, they tell us,
    At least so I've frequently heard,
But, "dosing" or "stuffing," those fellow
    Were up to each move on the board;
They got to his stall—it is sinful
    To think what such villains would do—
And they gave him a regular skinful
    Of barley—green barley—to chew.

He munched it all night, and we found him
    Next morning as full as a hog—
The girths wouldn't nearly meet round him;
    He looked like an overfed frog.
We saw we were done like a dinner—
    The odds were a thousand to one
Against Pardon turning up winner,
    'Twas cruel to ask him to run.

We got to the course with our troubles,
    A crestfallen couple were we;
And we heard the "books" calling the doubles—

A roar like the surf of the sea;
  And over the tumult and louder
    Rang "Any price Pardon, I lay!"
Says Jimmy, "The children of Judah
    Are out on the warpath to-day."

Three miles in three heats:—Ah, my sonny,
    The horses in those days were stout,
They had to run well to win money;
    I don't see such horses about.
Your six-furlong vermin that scamper
    Half-a-mile with their feather-weight up;
They wouldn't earn much of their damper
    In a race like the President's Cup.

The first heat was soon set a-going;
    The Dancer went off to the front;
The Don on his quarters was showing,
    With Pardon right out of the hunt.
He rolled and he weltered and wallowed—
    You'd kick your hat faster, I'll bet;
They finished all bunched, and he followed
    All lathered and dripping with sweat.

But troubles came thicker upon us,
    For while we were rubbing him dry
The stewards came over to warn us:
    "We hear you are running a bye!
If Pardon don't spiel like tarnation
    And win the next heat—if he can—
He'll earn a disqualification;
    Just think over *that*, now, my man!"

Our money all gone and our credit,
    Our horse couldn't gallop a yard;
And then people thought that *we* did it!
    It really was terribly hard.
We were objects of mirth and derision
    To folk in the lawn and the stand,
And the yells of the clever division
    Of "Any price Pardon!" were grand.

We still had a chance for the money,
    Two heats still remained to be run;
If both fell to us—why, my sonny,
    The clever division were done.
And Pardon was better, we reckoned,
    His sickness was passing away,
So he went to the post for the second
    And principal heat of the day.

They're off and away with a rattle,
    Like dogs from the leashes let slip,
And right at the back of the battle
    He followed them under the whip,
They gained ten good lengths on him quickly
    He dropped right away from the pack;
I tell you it made me feel sickly
    To see the blue jacket fall back.

Our very last hope had departed—
    We thought the old fellow was done,
When all of a sudden he started
    To go like a shot from a gun.
His chances seemed slight to embolden
    Our hearts; but, with teeth firmly set,
We thought, "Now or never! The old 'un
    May reckon with some of 'em yet."

Then loud rose the war-cry for Pardon;
    He swept like the wind down the dip,
And over the rise by the garden,
    The jockey was done with the whip
The field were at sixes and sevens—
    The pace at the first had been fast—
And hope seemed to drop from the heavens,
    For Pardon was coming at last.

And how he did come! It was splendid;
    He gained on them yards every bound,
Stretching out like a greyhound extended,
    His girth laid right down on the ground.
A shimmer of silk in the cedars
    As into the running they wheeled,
And out flashed the whips on the leaders,
    For Pardon had collared the field.

Then right through the ruck he came sailing—
    I knew that the battle was won—
The son of Haphazard was failing,
    The Yattendon filly was done;
He cut down the Don and the Dancer,
    He raced clean away from the mare—
He's in front! Catch him now if you can, sir!
    And up went my hat in the air!

Then loud from the lawn and the garden
    Rose offers of "Ten to one *on*!"
"Who'll bet on the field? I back Pardon!"
    No use; all the money was gone.
He came for the third heat light-hearted,
    A-jumping and dancing about;
The others were done ere they started
    Crestfallen, and tired, and worn out.

He won it, and ran it much faster
   Than even the first, I believe
Oh, he was the daddy, the master,
   Was Pardon, the son of Reprieve.
He showed 'em the method to travel—
   The boy sat as still as a stone—
They never could see him for gravel;
   He came in hard-held, and alone.

But he's old—and his eyes are grown hollow;
   Like me, with my thatch of the snow;
When he dies, then I hope I may follow,
   And go where the racehorses go.
I don't want no harping nor singing—
   Such things with my style don't agree;
Where the hoofs of the horses are ringing
   There's music sufficient for me.

And surely the thoroughbred horses
   Will rise up again and begin
Fresh races on far-away courses,
   And p'raps they might let me slip in.
It would look rather well the race-card on
   'Mongst Cherubs and Seraphs and things,
"Angel Harrison's black gelding Pardon,
   Blue halo, white body and wings."

And if they have racing hereafter,
   (And who is to say they will not?)
When the cheers and the shouting and laughter
   Proclaim that the battle grows hot;
As they come down the racecourse a-steering,
   He'll rush to the front, I believe;
And you'll hear the great multitude cheering
   For Pardon the son of Reprieve.

ARTIST PROFILE

Rex Newell sold his first painting when he was only fourteen years old, in a promising start to his artistic career. Born in Fredrickton, he moved to Sydney to learn his craft, studying for three years at the Parramatta Fine Art Society and a further five years at Sydney Technical College studying Commercial Art and Sign Writing.

Always fascinated by the Australian landscape, he has also studied and painted in Arizona for several years, and the early American West has been another love.

Described as a "contemporary" artist, Rex Newell also shows Romantic influences in his work. His most recent paintings have a softness and style that give them an emotion and sensitivity that is distinctively unique. Over the thirty years of his career to date, his work is recognised and valued all over the world. His paintings are included in the private collections of such notables as Prince Philip, the Duke of Edinburgh, Crown Prince Harold of Norway, and the President of Ireland. American actor John Wayne also collected his work.

Over the years Rex Newell has indulged his love of outback Australia through extensive travel, and it was this that inspired his first book *Outback Pubs of Australia*. This was very successful and was soon followed by his interpretation through art of *Favourite Poems of Henry Lawson*. *Favourite Poems of Banjo Paterson* is his third book and, like the others, shows his talent for the passionate yet subtle representation of his subjects.